DAUGHTER OF THE SUN

RACHEL SPENCE

THE EMMA PRESS

For Jack and Michael

ᆼ

THE EMMA PRESS

First published in the UK in 2025 by The Emma Press Ltd.
Poems © Rachel Spence 2025.

The right of Rachel Spence to be identified as the author of this work
has been asserted in accordance with the Copyright, Designs and
Patents Act 1988.

ISBN 978-1-915628-34-3

A CIP catalogue record of this book
is available from the British Library.

Edited by James Trevelyan.
Cover design by Emma Dai'an Wright.
Typeset by Emma Dai'an Wright.

Printed and bound in the UK by CMP Digital Print Solutions, Poole.

The Emma Press
theemmapress.com
hello@theemmapress.com
Birmingham, UK

CONTENTS

Reason is only an instrument, a pincer. We use it to handle a substance that is made of fire and ice

THE ORDER OF TIME, CARLO ROVELLI

Kepler flies thanks to his mother's magic... Einstein wonders what he would see if he could ride a ray of light.

WHITE HOLES, CARLO ROVELLI

There is a girl [who] can pause stars

JASON AND THE ARGONAUTS, APOLLONIUS OF RHODES

CALL & RESPONSE

Act 1

July 1976, your garden, midnightish.
Our worlds distilled to nothing save each other
and this bewildering heat. I hear you
padding down the stairs – morphine trickle
of a mother's footsteps – beg you to let me
stay while you find whisky, deckchairs.
The lawn is dry as a ship's biscuit, but we are
watered by the scent of your tobacco plants.
My winter's bone is being old enough to know
I don't know what you're thinking. Not even
when the owls come. Two, maybe three,
their beatless wings spellbound against
earth's pull. Ten seconds we'll remember
all our lives. We know it, even then.

July 1986, noonish. Our car's conked out
in the sun-cooked dip of a rollercoaster
B-road en route to Ascot races. Punctured
or overheated, two hours from AA rescue,
your grin mocking the Gods of tyres
and fan belts. *We'll treat ourselves to lunch*
you purr, in the posh restaurant on the hill.
I don't remember anything we ate
in that shady, foxglove-speckled garden
but I recall the friction of my pencil skirt
as I trudged behind you on the verge,
your dancer's calves powering up the slope,
shoulder blades jutting through damp silk,
the way your hips spelled smile.

October 2005, Venice. Six weeks after he left me
and *you're* the one who's grieving?
Excuse me while I slam the phone down.
I have pain to knead and other mothers to find
– the lagoon with her cloak of asters, the auntly moon.
You've smashed our covenant (I helped a bit)
to teach me one last lesson. The eight-year-old
begging a note to be excused from chapel.
We're Jewish, aren't we? Your atheism deep as tubas.
Don't come to me. Fight your own battles.
Instead, I learn the grammar of surrender.
Love, literature, my mother tongue – all lay down
arms at the first whiff of blood. And yet
my heart beats on – just as you knew it would.

January 2013, Commercial Street.

Traffic fumes cauterising the day to twilight.

I'm between a broken boiler and a visa

application for a country I can't afford to visit.

Your voice like stale water dammed too long.

You didn't come for Christmas and now

the neighbours think that we're estranged.

I'm done, Mum, really, done.

My phone sliding into the ninth circle

of disappointing daughters. The queue

for visas Babylonian – so many faces.

All with mothers! And once again you're

buzzing at my hip. *Darling, how's your boiler?*

And once again, we're on.

March. My lover's kiss has framed my day
with light. Spring's diligent percussion
greening the tree outside my window.
The words flow freely, stitching me
into the morning's warp and weft. I've never
told you, have I, that sometimes when I write
it feels like letting blood. What haven't you
told me? What have we never asked?
Not now, Mum. But your voice is different.
Old-lady fear fluttering like a baby bird's.
You waited how long before going to a doctor?
Lay not that flattering unction to your soul
that not your madness but my trespass speaks.
The day no longer numinous. But we're still on.

Act 2

April. The relief of finding you perched
on your hospital bed. Lipsticked and cashmered.
Defiantly undimmed. Twelve hours post-op
you've drunk them out of tea and think you'd like
to go now. Nurses calling you the Steve Redgrave
of patients. Your healing seeded centuries ago
making you tough as the ash trees fighting
their way through frost-bitten Polish soil,
hunger for a better life incubating
in clogged, shtetl light. And yes, I'm proud to be
your daughter. We've cared what the neighbours
thought since we were in the caves. My ancestral
grannies counted grapefruit spoons, possessed
small dishes shaped like avocados.

May. Shropshire's benign folds cradling
your farmhouse. I'm scrambling eggs as dawn
smears sherbet pink across the kitchen window.
It's strange with you upstairs. The dogs as well.
I drag them down to pee. The only whines
that you'll allow. I can't believe it's me
you want here. Though only you could ferret
my name out of a sacred text. *Jacob waited*
seven years for Rachel and I waited seven years
for you. (You've rejigged history all our lives.)
I'm terrified I'll hurt you when I change
your dressing but I am blushing
not at your scarred and holy absence
but at the way my hands are shaking.

May. St John's Hill, Battersea. The guarded
heat of summer rain like *sorry* on my skin.
Your call arrives while I'm en route to
the computer medic. You say you don't want
further treatment but can we go to Paris?
My skinny latte pooling on the pavement,
omertà between mother and daughter spilling
its secrets into the cracks. You'd tell all too
but I have never tortured you like this.
I want to smash my laptop on the road.
Passengers on a bus watching as I have watched
crazed people melting down on London streets.
Female Moses railing at Her Lady.
You will take your fucking tablets!

May. Still. My fifth espresso and it's not yet 10.
The silence between us scored by
a master builder. Notes of concrete.
Chords of blood and feathers. Noir edition
of those days when two of us together in a room
meant one of us was struggling to breathe.
Nothing has prepared us for this place.
Though I remember nights driving through
the cowled Welsh dark, your fairytales braiding
us tighter, tighter... The way we both hate spring –
its sharp, green birth pangs heralding so very little.
My father's name staining my screen like milk.
Could you go with your mother when she sees
her surgeon? And once again, we're on.

June. The doctor could be my younger sister.
Let's throw jealousy into our toxic mix.
A childless writer in my 40s, nothing I do
matters very much. But briefly, in this room,
I am a good daughter. You're the Scorpio
but she and I have trapped you in our pincer
movement. Papa's the poker player but we
are gambling like pros. She's bid you chemo
and you've called our bluff with zero treatment.
We'll call it quits at six weeks' radio –
I'll come down on my birthday. We drink to it
at Morrisons' caff – tea the colour of a rubbish
perm and carcinogenic doughnuts.
Outside it's summer. Your garden waits for us.

My birthday weekend. You're wag-tail happy
as I shamble in. Your kitchen's far too tidy.
Where is the unswept cottage light? Who washed
the cat hair off the cushions? Put ceanothus
on the table? Madonna-blue, whispering
that mother love is its own call and response.
The garden stirs and twitches like a river
pressing at its banks. Roses and hollyhocks
grown coltish with neglect. Your dream of controlled
wildness slipping into jungle night sweats.
You're making tea, denying soreness, sadness,
the shame of unknown fingers. *Move here. No, here.*
Good. Nearly done. But the dogs are quiet.
My father does not speak the whole weekend.

Your final check-up. August. Nimbus clouds
prised open by Delft blue. Waiting is hard.
The women serving tea and biscuits wear
survivors' smiles. This time we do not say
how young they are. How they could be me.
I know that I've inherited half your genes.
I drink my body weight in tea. Feel naked
without lipstick. But what of your stoic heart?
Your gift for loving men? That blowtorch smile?
They're calling us. The doc says we can bugger off.
Come back in two years' time.
We'd rather cut off our own hands than cry.
Let's celebrate at Morrisons.
Fancy a doughnut, Mum?

Interval

7.01am, May 2018. Your garden. Sun clotting
in the branches of a neighbour's maple, leaves
so dense the air around them cannot breathe,
their filigree sieving the beams as a mother's skirt
sifts the tears of her martyred son, the cloth pressed
to her cheek years after it has dried. I'm drinking
coffee, reading, writing poems, weaving myself
into a world where everything is still as it
should be: this beaten copper light, the clink
of china from the kitchen as Papa makes
the tea he'll take up to your room, a ceremony
that's lasted 60 years. No witness needed.
I cleave to caffeine, love and words. Time blinks.
And once again, we three triangulate.

Late May 2020, you and your garden
resisting lockdown beneath a thatch of birdsong
bristling with escapee coos, fugitive whistles,
your feral spirit bursting through *coups d'état*
of foxgloves, monkshood, salvia the colour
of pomegranates held by Christ Children,
their mothers gazing forwards to the Passion.
So once you gazed at me, so now I…
No, let's retell. My Madonna is a fighter
rejecting dead men's histories, watching
lemon light on sapling birches, the golden moss
of bumble bees, their delicate, obsessive turning,
learning to count time as grains that whirl
not flow, spinning us back to love's defiant zero.

Act 3

7.02am, acne of rain on the window,
rind of cellulite moon. From the kitchen
Bach's brisk exfoliations whisking me
back to last night as I rose and fell
in candlelit darkness, rootless shadows
begging for a foothold on the flame's
blue yolk. They say you should devote
your practice to someone who needs
your love or energy but in days
with more clamour than stars I pray
for one more morning, one more sonnet,
my father reading Lorca on the sofa,
terrier pooled on his lap like knitting,
his hair so long now, its residue of gold.

Ledge days. Leek-white. Unreckoned.
Love thickening like flour and milk
over our low blue heat. *If I hadn't*
been an academic, I would have been
a forester – my father as we walk
the Easy Access Path, my shock salting
the sunlight as it corrugates the pines'
grey verticals. When I tell Mum
she doesn't blink, her fingers crimping
pastry around the china birds that crown
her favourite pie dish. You dye each other
in a marriage. Take on each other's pigments.
Together you are purple, my king and queen
of pies and dreams. *He's always loved trees.*

Hinge week, between equinox
and change of hour. Waking to blue
the colour of stained-glass, tibia of plum,
persimmon. Dawn as free gift. Uncalendared.
By day I watch you sleep, summoning
your breath like a snake-charmer.
The terrier curled on your chest
like a conch, her tiny body rising
and falling with the ridge and furrow
of your rib-cage. On the edge of a black hole
time stands still. *But the hands of the clock*
in the Jewish quarter go to left from right.
And we too choose to live *slowly backwards.*
Not borrowed time but earnt.

Threshold days, clockless as the lives
of animals. Time repurposed into
a dam against itself. Our diary thrives
on counting out these undialled hours.
The dogs stay close now. You long
to see your tree peonies in flower.
A tingle in your hand. The peonies pout.
It's time to call in mercenary troops.
Petals flopped back like ballet slippers
left out in the rain. Oxycontin swoops
in on her black horse. *They're over before*
before they've begun, you mutter.
But in that quantum hinge, we made
an alphabet from love's ungrammared stutter.

Gnomon days, loss-fast.
Last night you came to me as rain,
your heartbeat tapping on the gutter,
faulty, persistent, curling your lip
as July unsummers through wilt
and droop. Not even your clematis
can purple this drenched morning.
Don't cry! You need to deadhead!
(Nothing bedraggled about your imperatives.)
You scoffed at my notion of a Garden
of Eden but I'm watching your lilies
as they cinder the mist, remembering that you
were a rule-breaker to your last fierce gasp.
We watched as you flew.

Act 4

Levee days, unleavened.
I remember swimming. Untrellised by heat.
Octaves of dog roses. Damselflies stapling
the reeds. At this hour, the river a convent
of untamed women with unshamed bodies.
Below the weir, the current counts us down
but we prefer to go in from above, the water
still as a stopped clock. Coiled time. Wishless
as kisses. Last breaths. Breathless. *Did you
see the kingfishers? No, I was talking to you.
Three passed right above your head.*
I don't care. Your blue is more brilliant than
any waterbird's. It's getting hard now.
But the midges are friendly. They cling to me.

Pirr days, unchatelained.
Who would have thought that we would
end up here? Suspended between your world
and mine. This is a thin place. Claustral.
Unstoried. Water less mother than midwife
and medium. *Who does pay the ferryman?*
Hush! Not now, Mum. I try to swim close
to the bank, eavesdrop on seances of alder,
reed, loosestrife, dragonfly. Love underwritten
onto the Teme's cool bed. Here, we rebirth
each other while the ducks snooze late because
they know everything and the red cow waits
for sunset when the castle unkeeps her ghosts
to walk behind you holding the train of your gown.

Thalweg days, unsounded.
Love flowing through our private heartseam.
At this hour the river a chapel where
mermaids kneel before drowned queens.
We've all lost someone. Grief smoking
through the ermine of mist, the bulrushes'
damp covert. Did you know that Teme
means 'dark one' in a Celtic tongue?
The castle nods. Once a confessional
for honeymoon riddles. Hymen or guillotine?
One fracture foretelling another. If I stretch
myself across the water's skin, will I see you
on the other side? Don't you dare tell me
that you're always with me. Swim!

Spannel nights, unrivered.
Loitering on the banks of my dreams, I want
to curl up with the ducks in the reeds' dewed
spiral but I've neither beak nor tailfeathers
to bury it in. If people ask I say you're still
with me, tough as a bramble, blooming
the darkness with your indigo smile.
But you're nearer when I don't have to imagine
the water as well. Who knew I'd struggle for breath
in grief's helical currents, miss you most
on days when I'm happy? Shouldn't a playbook
for loss contain language for absence?
Let's sit on the weir in the lee of our afterwords.
We'll kvetch about Boris; pretend we've seen otters.

Skerry nights, unsighted.
I'm shivering at the bus stop, the world
reduced to drizzle, tyre splash, chilled thighs.
This was your season: crisp, demanding,
sparked out of friction like the cicada's song.
Did you know one village saved itself
from the tsunami because somebody noticed
the cicadas had fallen silent? Do you know
everything now? Are you clairvoyant
as the river that runs through us, still, though
I haven't swum for months? Are you watching
as the bus snarls up, headlamps spitting
cinders in the rain, telling me to take a cab,
you'll pay? Is it time to move to higher ground?

Swale days, unravelled.
Shineless, swollen, lethal as liquid lead.
Our pool above the weir blocked by fallen trees
that floated downstream in the latest storm.
The heathen in you loved wild weather, cleaving
to Gower's rain-boiled seas and gale-burnt cliffs.
In Wales, the Dark Ages were golden years.
Your last months too were touched with glory.
Unlatched from time, we danced like *spiritelli*
carved by Donatello for a baptismal font
gleefully micturating, celebrating new life
in spindrifts, jets and pinwheels, spouting
defiance at death's parched clock, daring him
to dive as deep as we sprayed high.

Saltmarsh days, unwatered.
Struggling to find the poem in the morning,
the garden waking to the creak and clink
of shutters, my neighbour's taut croon
to her toddler. Had forgotten how May
clogs Venice with the scent of jasmine,
how a baby's cry is more cat than human.
This time last year we didn't know you had
just weeks to live. Sat in your garden
watching the hen pigeon plunge over
and over into your solanum unless
her chicks were yelping out her absence.
John Cage found music in the dust of silence.
My sonnet in your body dissolving into blue.

Thermocline days, unplumbed.
At this hour the river a secret, its stories
flotsammed through pollen, feathers, petals
of willowherb. The kingfisher greyed
by dusk though its blueless swoop is still
the sign of healthy water. We could do
with a sign, you and I, as the cormorant dives
to Jurassic time and the mayflies bend
the surface as they rise and land. Just one day
they're allotted yet they're older than dinosaurs.
Einstein found *witchery* in quantum time
but naiads need no occult clock.
We are our own go-between, the water
smooth behind us as if we'd never been.

Riprap days, unbreached.
Eighteen months without you and we're closer
than we've ever been. The river in full spate,
ransacking the bank for twigs, leaves,
sewage bubbles. Five hundred million
years ago this county lay under a shallow sea.
On Wenlock Edge the limestones nurture coral.
These days we understand the fury of deep time.
Sometimes I see egrets, capstoning the weir,
bewildered by what we've done to weather.
Sometimes Papa gets sick. Sometimes I do see
otters – somersault of muddy silk, whiplash of
tail quilled in cloudy ink. Sometimes I think
we're done. For now, the Teme keeps mum.

MEDEA'S SONG

There is a place with names for the wind

It is dawn

She remembers anvils
women running
    to beat the tide
palaces crumbling
    into feathers
The first time
    she noticed light
headland swaddled
    in mist, bandages
puddled in
    a basin, estuary
of brighter matter
    She remembers spindles
unsayable time

She will be unmapped

                      unread, unnumbered

     An untelling

The ship crying

all through the night, the women weeping

tears of amber

her aunt's wineless libations

Jason pulling her towards him

as an archer draws his arrow before he lets it

fly!

What was unsaid

        how much she loved the sea

That first journey on the Argo, rising before dawn
the water stirring as if an animal is trapped
beneath its folds

        cupped in the stern's curve, the sailors numb
        to her as if they know out here she's scoured
        of all she was – daughter, sister, princess, witch

        she's no-one's bride-to-be

out here, there's only newness
ferrous tongue of sea and sky
trembling, fibrous

        you watch and watch

but morning's shy as flowers –

their opening an inward turn
unscrolling of the mind's eye

      This is Gods' work   And yet, as dawn breaks

pieces of infinity over

      the Argo's sails   she feels the shudder of

      a different knowing

      Is that the scissor-kick of gull wings
      or just a trick of the light?

She will land on the other side of outrage
beyond murder, sacrifice
way beyond revenge

Others have come before her and others will follow
Not all will be seen but all will see each other, across
epochs, galaxies, light years, archives

Do not call them seers or sisters

They are the owls of history

nightfliers   outliers

wingbeats so slow they unhinge time

a quantum swiftness, porous as ash

They'll teach us to see in the dark

She is haunted by

poppies

stone bridles

love decomposed

to lines

on a spectrum

anger swarming

like

atoms

in a rock

unpunished   unforgiven

What was unsaid

how much she hated witchcraft

Dispatched to Hecate before first bleed

she learnt to read the landscape's private light
dark, wet, metallic   fog like wire wool
acne of pebbles on the littoral

those coffin trees
her tutor's belfry smile at snuffing out
a daughter of the sun

Always low tide

How much she envied Thetis –
her body *like a breeze or dream*
salty, kelp-eyed, soluble

as photons

always swimming
in and out
of other people's stories

What no-one told her

        That women are loved
        for listening, that love
        is like space, smooth
        from above, but when
        you're close it shatters
        and foams

This is the weave of the world, mesh-froth, *millefeuille*,
minute in its particulars

        undone
        gone
        no
        0
        oh!

What she was taught

> The stars are dead
> Time bends
> There are planets
> where she is
> still at home
> watching darkness
> hold shimmer
> like water
> Granular flicker
> as if there was a veil
> between herself
> and her

They pointed up to Heaven and told her
she would see remnants of light
left over from the Big Bang

>> Creation's chaff?

But she was watching the lavender haunches
of the sea rolling out time like dough

Thin, thinner. The wooden board shines through –
its grainy, unwashed gold

           Herb smells   Green spells

Skin that had never seen light
Thorns so sharp the air itself
grows brittle
Nothing is pliant

                  Sieve more
                          Dowse more

Love?

Love is a petrified angel

washed up by the green bone of the sea

Lady of coincidences, she rejects you!

Do not come here
with your taffeta lies, your gravitational mistakes

Her mistress is the queen of thresholds

Today, they are cooking the winds

She remembers cranes
their shy calligraphies
        on china, silk, cushioned
by snow-paper
        Proof if it were
needed that on the moon
        a feather and
a lead weight
        fall at the same speed
There's a place
        where epochs scatter
like beads on a rosary
        and you can hear cantos
for vanishing time
        Infinity's last act
Once, she hovered briefly
        on the horizon
 of a black hole
        returned to earth
to find millennia
        had passed

She remembers honeycombs
the corrosion of winter trees
        black chivvying blue out
to the sky's selvedge
        entropy's mad mutterings
Her dreams have been
        warehoused in the freeport
of a king's imagination
        But she hides
                in the wainscot

She remembers Orpheus
chords that have
        never known seasons
Archive her!
        A killed negative
who dared to slackline
        in an era of giants
Your bleating is
        a drumroll of silence
while she repairs
        her children's skin
with gold

Oh, how we coddled them!
        Those orphan quanta
How we lambed
    their sacrifice into
our dullard's crib
        Medea consigned
to history's portacabin
        For all maternity!
(Mother, he wrote)

What was unsaid

      how much she loved her father
                       sun's favoured child
      who taught her to weigh fire
      plait music out of time
                     and driftwood

                     With physics
     in your blood, you'll always fear the truth
     is only there to catch you out
                  live every hour
     as if the moment before earthquake
     a leaden prescience, glaze in the air
     that isn't heat

                (Dogs hated her)

She remembers
    autumn
her favourite season
    athletic light
hurdling the dunes
    shadows long and
supple as the dancers
    at her father's feasts
the echo of
    their footsteps
clasping time as stars
    despair
the edges of black holes
    You are
the wolf note now
    Aunt Circe speaking
truth to powerlessness
    But she's a seiche –
unheard bass tone
    of an inward ripple
(Dogs hated her)
    Have you guessed
her crime?

And yet at night
you'd find her
    on the beach
playing hopscotch
    in vertebrae
of moonlight
    Such tiny footprints!

Nobody drugged her

        under the clavicle of moon

    knuckle to knuckle

            SNAP!

   love like the wishbone of first light

      found with a ropey telescope

        when you are looking for
something else

She and Jason coupling on the threshold

unmyth

Her mother's absent, barely worth a line

        She gave Medea beauty   tinned,
                                      skinned and
                                      thinned

algorithm for privacy

sang lullabies she'd learnt from naiads

Sometimes, she scored the planets into octaves

click, click on her abacus

her ear tuned to the reedy arias of the void

                its boneless harmonies

Jason did nothing!

      Save let her cross the lintel of his smile

and beg for pharmakons

          but – nights with no vernacular
unrecorded

      he asked so little

What she was learning

      light leans
      time slips

         myth
            falling
                from
                    mouth
                        to
                            mouth
                    sailor
              weaver
          scientist
        witch

      why do we talk of the sun
      crossing the sky
      when it is we who move?

      Medea's tacking webs of absence
      across the corners of the cosmos

               Will they gather dust?

It's scaffold-lonely out here

                              on the edge

              of knowing

                     though Thetis gleams by

every now and then

Hinge days. March-coloured. Opaque

                      She will be

our Lady of verges
princess of the littoral
queen of skirtings

                         She will glow

   with the inward light of cinders

Does she remember Colchis?

Past lives as a daughter
                    sister
                        student

        slipping through
                            a bevelled pause

    Always she loved the silence

                        between two notes of music

        wingbeats
                        children's laughter

Her only crime was crossing the Hellespont
                    of a poet's imagination

Latch days   Scrubbed out

A world where women managed water
and still dishonour was survival's twin

but she remembers almond blossom
moulting through her father's hands

the milk of someone's voice at twilight

wave, oar, vitreous wind

Do I not have children?

do I not I not do I do not
do I not I not do I do not
do I not I not do I do not
do I not I not do I do not

NOTES

CALL & RESPONSE

p.5 – 'Lay not your flattering unction... my trespass speaks' is a rewording of the same line from *Hamlet*.

p.20 – The lines in italics are from *Zone* by Guillaume Apollinaire, translated by Samuel Beckett (Dolmen Press, 1972).

p.26 – Ludlow Castle hosted the honeymoon of Prince Arthur and Catherine of Aragon in 1501. After Arthur's death, Catherine married his brother Henry VIII, denying that her previous marriage was consummated. Later, Henry married Anne Boleyn on the basis that Catherine's marriage to Arthur was consummated.

p.29 – 'Gleefully micturating' is a rewording of a phrase used by A. Victor Coonin in *Donatello and the Dawn of Renaissance Art* (Reaktion Books, 2019).

DEFINITIONS

Levee – an embankment built to prevent the overflow of a river.

Pirr – a light breath of wind that makes a cat's paw on the water.

Thalweg – the line of greatest depth in a valley, often

used to describe the line of the deepest, fastest and therefore most erosive water in a river near the centre but towards the outer bank.

Spannel – Cornish word for calm patches of water in the lee of rocks where there is shelter from the tide and waves.

Skerry – a rocky island or reef, one that is usually submerged during high tide.

Swale – turbulent water; also the root of swallow, bird of swooping flight.

Saltmarsh – coastal wetlands that are flooded and drained by the tides.

Thermocline – a distinct layer in a large body of water in which the temperature fluctuates.

Riprap – human-placed rock or other material used to protect shoreline structures from water, wave, or ice erosion.

MEDEA'S SONG

p.45 – 'like a breeze or dream' from *Jason and the Argonauts* by Apollonius of Rhodes, translated by Aaron Poochigan (Penguin, 2014).

p.66 – 'Do I not have children?' from *Medea* by Euripides, translated by John Davie (Penguin, 2003).

ACKNOWLEDGEMENTS

Versions of some of these poems appeared in *Snakeskin, Dwelling During the Pandemic, PN Review, 14* magazine and *Call & Response*, my 2020 pamphlet with The Emma Press.

Enormous thanks to James, Emma, Georgia and Peri at The Emma Press for their skill, sensitivity, patience and imagination. Thanks to them, the production of *Daughter of the Sun* has been an unalloyed pleasure from beginning to end.

Thank you to those who read some or all of these poems, in particular Nadine El-Enany and Ella Frears. Their observations improved the book immeasurably.

Thank you to Mimi Khalvati who showed me how transformative poetic form can be – and how much fun it is to write.

Thank you to Emi Takahashi Tull – my still point in an unstable world.

Thank you to my tiny, irrepressible family, human and canine. You know who you are - the wind beneath my wings, sisters and brothers under the skin, living proof that blood isn't thicker than water, that Venice, yoga and wild swimming are recipes for happiness and that love is all that matters.

Finally, thank you to my mother. Then, now, always.

ABOUT THE POET

Rachel Spence lives in London, Ludlow and Venice. Her poems explore themes including time, absence, motherhood and water. She has published three pamphlets: *Furies* (Templar, 2016), *Call & Response* (Emma Press, 2020), and *Uncalendared* (Coast to Coast Journal Winner, 2023).

Her debut collection *Bird of Sorrow* (Templar, 2018) was highly commended in the 2019 Forward Prize. Her prose poem *Venice Unclocked*, in collaboration with photographer Giacomo Cosua, was published by Ivory Press in 2022. Her poetry has appeared widely, including on BBC's *The Verb*, and in *PN Review, The North, The London Magazine, 14* magazine and *Tears in the Fence*.

Her non-fiction book *Battle for the Museum*, which explores the relationship between art, power and money, was published by Hurst in 2024.

ABOUT THE EMMA PRESS

The Emma Press is an independent publishing house based in Birmingham. It was founded in 2012 by Emma Dai'an Wright and has grown to five part-time staff members following support from Arts Council England's Elevate programme in 2020-23.

The Emma Press specialises in poetry, short fiction and children's books, with translations across all genres. Recent publications have won the Michael Marks Illustration Award and been shortlisted for the CLiPPA and the Week Junior Book Awards.

In 2024 The Emma Press was a Regional Finalist for Small Press of the Year Award in the British Book Awards, as well as shortlisted for the Independent Publishers Guild's Alison Morrison Diversity, Equity & Inclusion Award.

The Emma Press is passionate about publishing literature which is welcoming and accessible

theemmapress.com

@TheEmmaPress